The Gifts of the Tarns

The two tarns lay in a fold of the hills, close by the cottage where the knife-grinder and his wife had their home. One, Tarn Leban, was fruitful and good: its waters sweet, its fish plentiful. The other, Tarn Tegrof, was poison to memory: the smallest drop drunk by man, woman or child would cause them to forget all they knew.

When the knife-grinder learned this, he determined never to touch anything from Tarn Tegrof. But his son, Tom, was curious; and when the tarns were frozen from end to end he set out to see what lay beyond Tarn Tegrof. Forgetful of the warning he drank from the lake, and instantly remembered nothing about his past.

This is the story of Tom's wanderings in a strange land of forgetfulness and his eventual return to a home he could not recognize.

The Gifts of the Tarns

ELISABETH RUSSELL TAYLOR

Illustrated by Mairi Hedderwick

COLLINS
St James's Place, London

William Collins Sons & Co Ltd
London · Glasgow · Sydney · Auckland
Toronto · Johannesburg

First published 1977

ISBN 0 00 184269 2

Made and Printed in Great Britain by
William Collins Sons & Co Ltd Glasgow

The Gifts of the Tarns is dedicated
to Tom Fairs

The Gifts of the Tarns

There was once a knife-grinder who travelled from village to village, sharpening knives and scissors, scythes, sickles and saws. He lived with his wife in a tinker's caravan drawn by a piebald horse. The couple had married a long, long time ago and when they were young had hoped for a child.

"When a child comes we shall settle," the grinder promised his wife, "but until such time we are travelling folk."

It was a hard life. The grinder was paid very little, even though the saws he sharpened cut through logs as though they were butter, and the scythes cut through thickets as if they were clouds of smoke.

On the first day of each month the grinder and his wife were to be found under the oak at Barleymill, the grinding-wheel set up by the side of the caravan, the piebald horse drinking contentedly at the village pond. While the grinder worked, his wife bought her bread from Seth's Bakery and her cheese from Ben's Village Stores and passed the time of day with the women of the village. But as the years stole by, without bringing the grinder and his wife a child, both grew sad and inward.

There were many villages on their route: Parsley Hay, Moonmint, Water's End and Crofters' Joy.

"When we have a child . . ." They used to play a game, settling in this village or that in their

STORES
BAKERY

minds, growing this vegetable and that flower, whitewashing the walls of the cottage, keeping a pig and a few chickens, building a fire in a real grate. And although they would set the game in Parsley Hay, Moonmint, Water's End and Crofters' Joy, each knew the other had determined on the ruined cottage that lay between the two tarns in the hills, Tarn Tegrof and Tarn Leban, five miles to the west of Barleymill. It was here that they set up camp on the first day of the summer months, when work brought the grinder to Barleymill and the days were long enough to travel into the village from the hills in the morning and back into the hills at night.

As the years followed more quickly, one upon the last, the grinder's wife still did not bear a child and their dream of settling faded. So too did their taste for the game, for company and for conversation. They prayed for a miracle, but like so many miracles it did not come when it was bid, and like so many people who pray only for miracles they ceased to pray when none occurred. The grinder's wife gave up hope and with it all pleasure in life. Her hair turned steely grey like a winter sea, her brow became furrowed like a winter field. She moved slowly, if at all. The grinder spent all the daylight hours working. He put aside the mouth organ that once he liked to play. He walked with his eyes down and his shoulders humped.

One summer's day the grinder had taken the horse on to Moonmint green for a day of knife sharpening and had left his wife in the caravan in a clearing in the forest on the outskirts of the village. Now that she had no taste for human company she kept the company of trees and creatures in the glades. She watched motionless as squirrels clambered over the exposed roots of the trees and tits darted like tiny coloured arrows through the branches. It was usual for the grinder to find his wife seated in the same position when he returned at night as he had left her when he set out in the morning.

On this summer's day the woman found herself wandering down to the stream. She watched as fish burst circles on the still surface of the water. When the sun had risen high and its rays struck her back she caught sight of her face reflected in the watery mirror. She observed it was more rounded than she remembered it; it was not for many years that she had looked at herself in a looking glass, and when last she had she was a young woman – tall, slim and lithe. She stood staring down into the water and was lost in wonder. She passed her hands over her cheeks and her breasts and her belly and found herself to be full and rounded. The woman spent the whole morning by the water examining her reflection from all angles and then looking back at her body. She felt the weight of sorrow lift like a morning mist.

As the grinder rode back through the green gloom of the pine forest he sensed something special on the air. His heart was light and his back was straight. He smelt pine cones burning and heard a faint crackling. As he rounded the corner and came to the clearing in the forest where he had left his wife, he saw she had made a fire in the brazier and that a cauldron was balanced over the flames. His wife heard the clip-clop of the horse's hooves on the dry path, jumped down from the caravan and ran towards her husband.

"We are to have a child! We are to have a child!" she cried out breathlessly, in the greatest possible wonder and delight. The grinder leapt from his horse and tied his wife about with his arms. For the first time in many years they laughed with happiness.

And so it happened at last that their life changed. And because the miracle had taken time to come about it would be the more precious when its promise was fulfilled.

Next morning the grinder drove the caravan over the hills in the direction of Barleymill. It was a four-day journey even though they made only brief stops to eat and sleep. At Barleymill they stocked up with food at Ben's Village Stores and all they needed to make good the ruined cottage. They paid for their requirements from the savings they had put by from the first days of their marriage, and had kept hidden behind the panelling in the caravan.

First the grinder replaced tiles on the roof

and saw to it that the chimney was clean and would draw out the smoke from the range. His wife whitewashed the walls of the two small rooms that crouched beneath the roof and were to serve as bedrooms for themselves and their child. She mixed a concoction of herbs with which to kill the beetles that had eaten into the oak staircase that struggled from the kitchen to the rooms above, and another of beeswax and lavender to clean and polish the wood until it was smooth and shone like ripe conkers. As fast and as carefully as a bird builds its nest in spring to be ready for a clutch of eggs, the couple made their home to be ready for the arrival of their child.

When all was complete, the cottage set like a stage for a performance, the grinder returned to his craft, and worked not only all the hours of the day but many hours of the night, grinding knives and tools. He was obliged to leave his wife alone in the cottage for three and four nights at a stretch to earn money to buy wool and linen for the child, to put aside the price of the services of the midwife who would deliver the child, to buy oil lamps and two comfortable chairs to set beside the range and some new pots and pans.

His wife was content, alone in the cottage that rose small and firm between the two mountain tarns. Each time her husband returned he brought with him a new object to garnish their home and a few materials the farmers gave him from which to make shelves, a table, a bench and a chest for the child's clothes and blankets. When the chest was full of tiny garments sewn and knitted, and blankets woven on the hand loom, the woman's time arrived.

The grinder hastened to Barleymill. He called at the midwife's cottage and told her to make herself ready to return with him that evening to his cottage that lay between the tarns.

As the grinder and the midwife drove out of the village into the hills, they talked. The grinder spoke lovingly of the beauty of the land that lay in folds around the cottage and told the midwife of the changes he had wrought in the cottage.

"I have never been out your way," the midwife told the grinder. "No one's settled there in living memory. They don't dare. You're a brave couple . . ." Her voice trailed off in the direction of her unspoken thoughts.

The grinder agreed the cottage was remote but hardly thought it an act of courage to live there. He was poor; there was no alternative. "We are not brave folk," he said, "we are poor folk."

"Have you not heard the legend of Tarn Tegrof?" There was terror in the midwife's voice as she asked. The grinder had to admit that he had not heard the legend.

As the two strangers swayed through the night behind the piebald horse, the woman told the once-travelling man what all the villagers knew.

"Many thousands of years ago the land round Barleymill was flat. One day, far, far back in history before tales were written down, the earth trembled, thundered and split open. It threw its insides out. These hills are the entrails of the world. You will have noticed no villager ventures into the hills beyond the tarns. True, they have little time, and lack curiosity, but it must be said that the real reason is that they are afraid. 'We let the hills be; the hills let us be.' That is how they put it. When there is a thunderstorm, ancient memories of the origin of the hills spring to mind as the hills themselves sprang from the contents of the earth. The tarns formed at the same time. Now, Tarn Leban is a good lake and you can safely eat the fish that breed in it and the duck that swim on it. But Tarn Tegrof is a bad lake. Its waters are poison to memory. If any man, woman or child drinks so much as a cowslip's bell of water from Tarn Tegrof he forgets his very name."

It was November and the air was sharp as lemons. The midwife drew the horse blanket round her shoulders; the legend was as biting as the night air. She continued: "You must be vigilant and mark my words. Do not take fish, fowl or water from Tarn Tegrof; do not gather flowers for the table and herbs for the pot or reeds to dry to seat your chairs. You risk to lose all you have. If you forget who you are, forget you have a wife and now perhaps a child, forget the details of your existence, what would be left to you? Do not be tempted to reach the hills beyond Tarn Tegrof; temptation is a wicked thing." The midwife shuddered.

"I shall always remember what you have told me." The grinder spoke solemnly. "We shall take all we need from Tarn Leban and resist the temptation of the hills beyond Tarn Tegrof. However abundant the produce of Tarn Tegrof we shall not touch it."

That night the grinder's wife gave birth to a son. The full moon smiled. They named the boy Tom.

The grinder and his wife were happy. The cottage gleamed with colour; the land around the cottage became fertile. From Tarn Leban they took water; it was pure and good. They took fish to eat and herbs to flavour their food. They picked rushes and flowers and dug channels to irrigate paddy fields for rice. They kept a pig, which worked hard munching all day and cleared an acre of land for them on which they grew vegetables. They kept chickens, in a manner of speaking for it was really the chickens that kept them: the birds pecked off the untilled land and in return laid well, and eventually gave themselves up to the pot. The grinder worked less at his wheel as his small-holding developed; he spent the spring and summer months on the land with his wife, for that was when the land most needed his attentions. During the winter months he journeyed round the villages sharpening knives and tools.

Tom was a happy baby and a constant source of wonder and pleasure to his parents. Soon he was a year old and able to crawl round the kitchen and out into the yard. The couple's one anxiety was to keep the child away from Tarn Tegrof.

"If only it were not so vast," the grinder complained to his wife, "I would build a wall around it to keep Tom safe." But the tarn was as vast as an inland sea. Indeed, it seemed limitless.

The grinder built his son a coracle which he kept moored to a pole in Tarn Leban. As soon as Tom was old enough he learnt to do all his parents did; he played at working and enjoyed it. He took the coracle out into the deep waters of the good tarn and sat there with his willow rod and fished for the family. He drew water from the tarn, collecting it in two buckets he carried across the field to the cottage on the ends of a stout pole. At first he used small buckets but as he grew he was proud to manage heavier loads.

Mother, father and son understood and loved one another and the world in which they lived. They wanted for nothing because their needs were modest. As Tom grew older he was able to be an equal partner in managing the crops with his mother and humping logs with his father. Independently, he caught fish and snared rabbits. His father taught him the grinder's craft and sometimes the boy accompanied him on trips to outlying villages; he helped with the work so that his father was not obliged to spend nights away from home. Tom loved the tune made by the turning wheel. He loved the sight of the sparks that rose from the sharpening blades: tiny stars on which to wish.

Occasionally, Tom left his father at his grinding-wheel on the village green and set off with a hone in his pocket to sharpen the farmers' sickles and scythes. He wondered as he walked by the village school what it was the village children learnt there all day. His mother had taught him to read and write and darn his socks. He could add, subtract and divide all the numbers he needed. He could invent stories, write them down and illustrate them. He could cook and wash the pots and clean the cottage, and he knew how to raise and care for plants and animals. He did not envy the village children cooped up like their chickens all day while he was free as a song-bird.

There was just one secret he did not share with his parents. He had a companion who fished with him on Tarn Leban!

One early morning as Tom sat in the coracle watching the mist rise off the water and settle like a magic carpet over the tips of the rushes, he noticed an orange cat sitting in a scooped-out log floating some distance away. The cat was leaning over the side of his log-boat, fishing in the clear water with his paw. He worked very quietly and stealthily. After this first encounter Tom often saw the cat and the cat often saw Tom, but each had his fishing to do and neither spoke, for had they spoken they would have frightened the fish away.

Tom enjoyed the seasons for the changes they brought, but winters in the hills were often hard. The snow fell thick and white from the lowering, grey sky and the tarns froze. Sometimes the grinder's wife and her son were cut off from the village of Barleymill and the knife-grinder for weeks at a time.

The cold of one such winter not only enveloped the land, but pierced to the hearts of the grinder and his wife. The grinder said goodbye to his wife and Tom, and was about to set off for Parsley Hay. He said he would visit all the outlying farms and return in five days' time. As he prepared to leave, the sky lowered until it pressed against the chimney of the cottage. "There'll be snow," he observed and wrapped himself round with a blanket over his coat.

Tom went out into the yard to the side of the cottage and threw a tarpaulin over the logs and peat, stacked in readiness against the winter cold. He pulled the coracle out of the water and laid it bottom up beside the logs. He went round the bins in which the family stored their provisions and made sure there was enough of everything to see them through a hard winter. "We need more sugar, father," he said.

"I'll buy sugar and currants for our Christmas

pudding when I get to Parsley Hay."

Tom stood at the door of the cottage and watched until his father disappeared over the brow of the hill. He and his mother sat in the grey light and were silent.

During the afternoon snow fell; during the night the temperature dropped and it became shiveringly cold. Tom kept the fire in. Next morning dawned crystal bright; winter tears hung at the windows and a thick sheet of ice lay across Tarn Tegrof. As the cold persisted the ice thickened and a choir of gulls collected.

Now, at last, thought Tom, I shall be able to discover what lies at the other side of Tarn Tegrof. I shall walk across the ice. It will be quite safe; it is so cold the ice could not possibly thaw for weeks.

Tom knew that his mother would not welcome his proposal and he searched for words with which to reassure her. She sat thinking quietly as he spoke: it was true that the tarn was well frozen and set firm for weeks to come. The boy did not plan to climb into the hills beyond the tarn, only to see how they looked. It was just a feeling she had, she could not explain it. But eventually she resigned herself to his assurances and was confident that his understanding of the changing patterns in the weather would guide and protect him. She packed him food and a flask of hot milk and put them in the canvas satchel he took with him when he journeyed. She watched him lovingly as he wrapped himself warmly in sweaters and boots and a thick coat and then, in imitation of his father, a blanket. The blanket had a round hole in the middle, through which he put his head. It reached to his knees and he secured it with coarse string round his waist.

"Go safely, my son," the woman said, handing Tom his satchel to sling across his chest. "I too would like to know what lies beyond Tarn Tegrof but I lack your courage to find out."

It was impossible to walk round Tarn Tegrof. Great rushes rose to a height of fifteen feet at the water's edge. Tom's feet crumped over the snow-covered field that lay between the cottage garden and the clotted rushes at the water's edge. Such view of the far end of the tarn that could be had from the cottage was as remote as if it had been sighted from the wrong end of a telescope. In the distance water and land were indistinguishable.

The grinder's wife stood at the door of the cottage and watched as her son strode on to the ice. She observed that he walked like his father and that he was tall for his fourteen years. As she turned and shut the cottage door behind her she felt an icy cold slice through her body like a knife. She turned back quickly, opened the door and called out, "Tom! Tom!" but the wind was driving from the east and carried her voice over Tarn Leban, and her son did not hear her as he walked across Tarn Tegrof. She noticed an orange cat she had never seen before step on to the ice. The woman turned back into the cottage, settled in the chair by the range and picked up her needle and thread.

Tom liked solitude. He had noticed that it was

when he was alone that he brought into rhyme what he saw with how he felt. He strode across the ice confidently. He ran and slid. He stopped and turned to look back at the cottage; it was already out of sight but he fancied he saw a curl of smoke rising in the sky between the tarns. He continued on his way walking, running and sliding across the ice until, in mid-tarn, he came upon a huge clump of rushes rising from the wrinkled, frozen waste. Ravenous sparrows were collected, conferring in the branches of the only vegetation within sight. Tom noticed how, as their beaks opened in complaint their breath escaped in tiny clouds on the raw air. He crumbled some bread; the birds left the rushes for his fingers where they perched to eat from the palm of his hand.

It was while he was examining grasses embedded in frozen water, like flies in amber, that he heard the plaintive, anguished cry of the gull. The sound came from the innermost depths of the clump of rushes. Tom thrust his way through the dense, tall stems. As he did so, his face was cut by leaves which, in their death,

were sharp as knives. He found a gull on the ice bed, one foot imprisoned in an icy trap. He took a knife from his pocket and gently eased the ice round the foot of the gull. The ice here was not solid and as the gull's foot was freed Tom saw how a few fish had survived in a patch of water that had remained unfrozen round the base of the rushes.

The gull shook its feathers and swept high into the sky. Tom observed the ecstatic flight of the rescued bird. As he looked down he saw his hands were covered with blood from the scratches the leaves had made on his face. He bent down and from the hole he had made in the ice he took water and washed his face. Cold stemmed the flow of blood. He cupped his hands and gathered more water and drank. As he did so a thunderbolt burst on his mind: this was Tarn Tegrof whose waters were poison to memory! He walked on across the tarn led by the freed gull that wheeled and swooped above his head. "I wonder what I am doing here?" he said to himself – out loud. But since he had forgotten from where he had come, it hardly mattered where he was or where he was going.

Tom stepped off the ice and surveyed the banks of the tarn. Had he been able to remember the grassy verges that bordered the tarn near his cottage he would have been surprised at the difference. These banks were steep, made from huge slabs of grey stone. He clambered up and over the bank and looked around. The hills rose as high as mountains; they were matted with stunted pine trees. Tom saw that a path lay between the hills and walked towards it. The air was thick, so thick that as he breathed in, Tom feared he might choke. He thought he could hear distant music . . .

He looked back. The path behind him looked just the same as the path that lay before him: a stony scar between two great hills. But whereas trees managed to scratch a poor living on the hills facing the tarn, fewer and fewer survived in the landscape that stretched before him. As he walked, it got hotter and hotter and the land flattened out. Everything was grey. Then suddenly and unexpectedly a streak of orange flashed past Tom. It was a cat! But since Tom had lost all memory of what lay behind the tarn, he did not know that this was his companion who had fished in Tarn Leban. Nevertheless, he was delighted to have company in this forlorn land.

On and on he picked his way over the stony ground, led by the orange-coloured cat. Steam rose from cracks between the stones and the couch-grass that put out fragile strands above the ground had dried to straw in the heat. There were one or two scrubby bushes with sharp prickles and wizened grey berries. The only colour in Tom's world at that time was the orange of his companion's coat. What a cheerful colour, Tom thought.

The path went on and on. The stony land continued flat. Tom walked and walked. He took off his shirt and packed it into his satchel, and as he did so he came upon an apple and half a sandwich. He ate the apple, sitting rather uncomfortably on a pile of hot stones. The cat sensibly made himself comfortable on the satchel, and ate the cheese filling from the remains of the sandwich.

They had not gone much farther when Tom saw on the horizon a group of stone hives, tall and broad, facing on to a clearing. Several small children were playing there, they were rather dusty and grey. The cat walked towards the children, and the children were delighted and ran up to the cat and stroked him and said, "What a lovely cat! What a lovely cat you are!"

Tom could see that the stone hives were houses but they seemed to be deserted.

"Do you live all alone?" Tom asked the children.

They laughed. "We are always alone during the day; our parents are at work at the castle."

Tom learnt from the children that he was in the Kingdom of Op, that these were the children of King Op's slaves, who lived in stone hives outside the castle walls."

"Is the castle far away?" Tom asked a small boy.

"Not as far away for you as it is for me. Your legs are longer than mine."

One of the children gave the cat some cool milk to drink, and another gave Tom some water. Then they all said goodbye and Tom and the orange cat set off in the direction of King Op's castle.

When Tom first caught sight of the castle he was amazed by its size and shape and colour. Hordes of gardeners worked in the formal gardens. Some carried spades and dug, others worked with secateurs, sprays and hoes. Some pushed wheelbarrows, others pulled lawn-mowers. Tom saw giant dahlias, lilacs and mimosa being cut and laid in flat baskets, whilst daisies growing on the lawn were cut out and burnt on bonfires. The gardeners worked continuously and silently.

The castle was so huge he could not see its whole extent from where he stood. What he could see was composed entirely of circles. The windows were round, the doors were round,

the minarets that glistened in the sunlight were round and revolved, and from them poured a steady stream of music. In niches arranged by every door sat animals. Tom could not make out what they were, whether they were real or clockwork. From time to time a roar, a bark, a purr and a croak accompanied the music from the minarets. The fabric of the castle seemed to be composed of a mosaic of tiny coloured stones. Round the castle was slung a broad belt of silvery water.

As Tom walked up the drive that led to the main door, he noticed that it too was full of circles: the box trees that lined the drive had been clipped into ball shapes. The trunks of the trees were artfully concealed and the leafy balls appeared to hover a few inches above their round beds. Between the trees smaller beds were filled with green, exotic flowers. A number of bridges spanned the moat and led to different parts of the castle. All were transparent. Tom crossed the largest that led to the main door; it was slung so low across the water he had the impression of walking on the water itself.

The front door was flung wide open and the vast hall was athrong with the company of very round people, all laughing and being jolly. Tom stood at the threshold watching. He had hardly been there long enough to examine six people, when a very fat man with very red cheeks came up to him and handed him a gold platter on which was a cake and a round glass of ambrosia. "You are not eating; you are not drinking!" the man complained, as if there were something unnatural about both.

"I've only just arrived," said Tom, by way of explanation. He thanked the fat man for the cake and the drink and as he cautiously cut into the creamy fruity-scented delicacy he asked the man: "Are you having a party?"

"We are always having a party!" the man replied. He was a very nice man, Tom thought, very happy and welcoming.

As Tom continued to examine the people around him he felt uncomfortably conspicuous – he was so thin and oddly dressed by comparison.

Observing his discomfort his new friend suggested providing Tom with clothes similar to his own. "Let me get you something comfortable to slip into," he said, expansively, "hose, and a cope would suit you well, I think." So saying, he sized Tom up and disappeared into the crowd.

All around Tom, people danced and sang and ate and drank and laughed and played.

"And now, permit me to introduce myself," said the fat man who had returned with purple silk stockings, a magnificent gold brocade cope, lavishly embroidered, a silk shift to go beneath it and soft leather slippers for Tom's feet.

"I am King Op. The people you see around you are all members of the royal family – except those doing the work. They are my slaves. They were not born hereabouts . . ."

Tom recognized from King Op's tone that not being born hereabouts was a disadvantage and he started to wonder whether he had been born hereabouts, but he had to stop considering the matter because he had no memory. He put on the clothes King Op had brought for him.

As he fitted the shift the king produced some

cushions with straps attached: "Tie these inside your cope; give yourself some size, dear boy!" Tom did not like to refuse. When the king saw Tom dressed to his near satisfaction (for Tom was still too thin for his complete satisfaction, even with cushions) he hung gold and silver chains round his neck, pinned brooches to his cope and called his daughter (who was occupied doing a little dance with some other young people) and presented her to Tom. "This is my daughter, the princess," said King Op, swelling with pride. "You will love her; we all love her. Don't we, m'dear?" So saying, the king squeezed the princess's cheek between his fingers and made rather a silly face at her. Then he wandered off to be agreeable to other people and left Tom and the princess alone.

"You were doing such a pretty dance," observed Tom, "I really don't feel I should interrupt you."

"I have been dancing all my life; I can dance for the rest of my life," replied the princess, grandly.

"Do you dance all day?" asked Tom, rather

at a loss to know what to talk about.

"Of course!" exclaimed the princess. "We play and we eat; we dance and we sing. When night falls we sleep on mounds of rose petals to the sound of clockwork nightingales."

Tom listened carefully to the words of the princess and thought hard about what she had said. It puzzled him: something tugged at the back of his mind, but he lacked memory to assist it to the front.

"What do the slaves do all day?" he asked.

"They work. They keep the palace clean and warm and beautiful. They grow and cook our food. They cultivate the flower gardens. They paint our pictures and write our music and our stories. Some go off into the world and buy silks and satins for our clothes and dig for precious stones for our ornaments. I believe it is all very tiresome and very tiring for them."

"How interesting their lives must be!" said Tom, enthusiastically.

"Interesting!" gasped the princess. "Their lives are absolutely awful – which is what makes ours so absolutely lovely!"

The princess took Tom into the library and showed him the king's collection. "A mile and a half!" she said with satisfaction.

All the books were bound in soft white leather, tooled with delicate patterns, lettered with gold leaf and lavishly illuminated. But many of the volumes lacked words.

"Why don't these books have writing?" asked Tom.

"There are not as many soothing stories of luxury and delight as there are books in which to write. We cannot tolerate anything sad or nasty in the Kingdom of Op."

While the princess offered this explanation to Tom her fingers were idly peeling silver leaf from the walls of the library. "Most of our walls are finished with gold leaf. I really don't know why the king bothers with silver leaf in the library. I suppose it was all a whim of one of the court decorators. Silver, you know, is less precious than gold."

Tom had to admit that this was something he did not know. He told the princess that he liked the colours equally. "I like gold," he said, "because it is the colour of the sun. I like silver because it is the colour of the moon."

"What a curious young man you are!" mused the princess, taking a few steps back in order to view him better. "*I* like silver because it buys things, and I like gold better because it buys more things."

Tom had been living at the castle for many months. Just how many he did not know for nobody at the castle counted time and he had long ago given up keeping his own record. After the first days of his arrival, when he was both curious about the castle and determined not to stay long, he had felt no sense of urgency. He had grown lazy and indifferent; only the company of the orange cat aroused his tender feelings.

The king and his family made every effort to please Tom and keep him in their midst. They were attentive and generous to him but King Op was ever mindful of the fact that Tom was very different from the royal family. Difference worried and indeed irritated the king, and as he scrutinized Tom he took comfort from the boy's expanding girth, his developing taste for food, drink, dance and play and his flagging concern with all that lay beyond the gates of the castle.

"It is my dearest wish," the king told Tom, "that you and the princess should one day marry."

Tom felt flattered and since he was not expected to marry the princess right away he was able to toy with the idea along with other ideas of possessing works of art, jewels and yet more silks and satins. However, for the time being his attention was almost entirely centred on the orange cat.

Tom and the cat were always together. Tom fed the animal on morsels of caviar, smoked flying-fish and larks' tongues. He had arranged for one of the court decorators to spray the cat gold and mark it with bronze spots. Thus he obtained for his delight an exotic leopard-cat.

One day, as he led the animal round the fountain in one of the inner courtyards on a lead of platinum and gold thread, his attention was caught by the bubbles that frothed on a basin of silvery water. He thought how elegant the cat would look with a necklace of silver set with bubbles of moonstone that would catch the light as the animal stalked in the sun. No sooner had the thought risen in his mind than Tom led the leopard-cat in the direction of the workshops where the silversmiths and jewellers sat all day making beautiful ornaments for the king and his family.

The workshops were underground. They fitted together like the cells in a beehive. In tiny ill-lit booths, men and women worked all the hours of the day and night embroidering, sewing, cutting stones, working leather and weaving cloth. In further booths, men sat crossed-legged pounding herbs and spices gathered from all over the world to make one of a thousand different flavours to excite the palate of the king. Tom watched as an old woman, a pile of fruit before her, sat peeling, seeding and cutting huge fruits into dice the size of a pea. The fruit salad she was making,

she had been making all her life, and would continue to make until the day she died. It was eaten daily at the castle. The air underground was heavy, the noise was deafening and there was litter in the lanes. Tom eventually found the silversmith and described to him just what he had in mind for the leopard-cat. The silversmith drew a rough sketch of the finished article and Tom was exceedingly gratified.

"I shall return for it tomorrow morning," Tom said, rather grandly.

The silversmith looked uncomfortable and sought for words to explain to Tom that the necklace could not be ready by tomorrow morning. "I very much regret, sir," he said, "I shall not be ready quite so soon. My tools need sharpening and the knife-grinder is not expected for a few days . . ."

As Tom's mind and body had degenerated, his desire for food and drink and baubles had increased. He could not possibly wait for a few days! It was out of the question! If the knife-grinder was not expected to visit the silversmith for a few days, the silversmith must go to the knife-grinder – and take his tools with him and what was more Tom would go along too, right away!

Tom and the silversmith and the leopard-cat made their way through the narrow lanes bordered by the servants' quarters and the craftsmen's booths, the kitchens and the repair shops, until they reached the foundry. Men were at work in loin-cloths at the white-hot furnaces. To one side in the comparative cool, sat the knife-grinder at his wheel, a huge pile of domestic knives, farm tools, dressmaking scissors and gardening implements by his side.

The silversmith politely inquired whether the grinder would be so kind, whether he had a moment to spare, whether it would be possible and added how greatly it would be appreciated if the grinder would sharpen his few tools. The knife-grinder stopped the wheel and put down the tools on which he had been working. Very gently, with appropriate hand instruments, he straightened and sharpened the delicate tools of the silversmith's craft.

Tom stood watching, fascinated. In him there

stirred strong feelings. He would like to be straightening and sharpening those tools, to have the feel of metal in his hand, to run the points along his palm and the blades against his cheek. Finally, just before leaving, Tom passed the grinder his pocket knife and as the grinder turned the wheel and sharpened the blade against it, sparks flew into the air. Tom was transported! He could not identify what it was he thought or felt, he could not give it a name, but it was urgent and he knew he must leave the castle – quickly.

"I'll be going now," he said to the silversmith.

"The necklace will be ready for you tomorrow morning, sir."

"I shall not be needing it," said Tom.

The silversmith was not altogether surprised. The king and his family were capricious too. Things wanted urgently in the morning were often forgotten by evening. And so it was that he accepted Tom's abrupt change of mind – and yet quite misunderstood the reason for it.

Tom picked up the cat and made his way back through the network of passages that linked the underground workshops with the castle above. He noticed he was tired. He found himself in an unfamiliar courtyard and walked through an arch into a small, empty room, the walls of which were lined with looking glasses, the floor covered with plump cushions. He sat down to rest, the leopard-cat beside him. He stroked the animal. As he flattened the fur towards the cat's tail the gold paint shone brilliantly; as he brought his hand back towards its head, against the lie of the fur, he rediscovered the orange-coloured cat beneath. Tom looked into the green eyes of his friend and decided he looked best in his own coat. He brushed him free of paint.

"A cat is a cat, after all," he said to himself, "not a leopard."

He stood up and examined himself this way and that in the looking glasses. He pulled the turban from his head and the cope from his back. He removed the padding the king had insisted he wore. He pulled off the pointed leather slippers, the purple silk hose, the silk shift and all the chains and pins that decorated his chest and went in search of the clothes in which he had arrived at the castle. Only the king would know where they had been put. Tom went towards the great hall where the mid-day concert was in session.

The king was seated on his elaborate throne, his family all about him. "Dear boy!" cried the king, seeing Tom enter the hall, "you are not eating, you are not drinking, you have nearly missed the opening bars and where, oh where are your castle clothes?" His voice rose in a royal whine. With a flourish of his right hand the king indicated in one gesture that the music should commence, that Tom should be given food and drink and that he should sit down by the royal side. Tom explained that he had decided to leave the castle and that he needed his own clothes to wear.

"Of course you will want to leave – one day!" said the king, trying to sound reasonable, "but not today," he added, "not when the music's about to begin."

"My clothes . . ." Tom said, quite firmly. The king understood that Tom had made up his mind. He clapped his hands and a slave darted away to find Tom's clothes.

"I am mortified," the king cried, "mortified that you should wish to abandon us!" He turned to the princess: "Say something, m'dear, something to make him change his mind."

But the princess was busy with music and ice-cream and plans for a new tiara. Idly, she picked up Tom's cat. "I would like you to leave me your cat," she said, holding it out in front of her, examining it this way and that. "I think it might be amusing to own a hedgehog cat. I shall instruct the silversmith to make a spike-mail coat of bronze."

"I'm very sorry indeed, princess," Tom said quickly, "but I cannot possibly be separated from my friend."

"Dear boy," the king said, sadly, for now he could see that Tom was really leaving and leaving soon, "I would like to make you a present to remind you of us all when you are hungry and sad and cold in the outside world." He swept his hand round indicating both the beauty and luxury of the surroundings at the castle and how Tom might choose anything he liked to take along on his journey. "A diamond perhaps? A picture? A vase? One of the hounds? The princess?"

By now Tom had become so familiar with the voice of the king, and so unmoved by the list, that he barely noted he had been offered everything from things to animals to a person! But he knew that the possession of any one of the items suggested by the king would not have brought him happiness. "I would very much like a hone," he said.

"A hone!" exclaimed the king. "And what, if I may be so bold, is a hone?"

Tom informed the king that a hone was a stone on which to sharpen knives.

"Oh, well," the king confided, "I would hardly know about that sort of thing. Do we have one in the castle?" As he asked, he clapped his hands.

"A hone. At once!" he said to a slave. It was the first time he had used the word and he rather liked the sound so he repeated it three times.

Meanwhile Tom pulled on his old sweater and trousers which the slave had returned. He folded his coat and placed it on the blanket, drew the four ends of the blanket together, tied them with string and slung the bundle and his satchel over his shoulder.

Within a few minutes the slave returned with a hone balanced on a silver platter.

Tom observed how silly the tool looked, robbed of its dignity. "It's a lovely object in use," he said, feeling that he must come to the defence of the object.

The king picked up the stone as if it were a piece of sculpture. He held it between his fingers, stroked it, smelt it, touched it with the tip of his tongue, shook it and, with an expression of surprise and disappointment, handed it to Tom.

"Well, it's certainly nothing to look at. It doesn't smell or taste good, it has no sound. Are you quite sure it is exactly what you want?"

"Quite sure," said Tom, politely. "I shall be able to earn my living with it in the outside world."

"Do what!" exclaimed the king as if Tom had said something improper and insulted his host.

There was no point in trying to explain, thought Tom. He thanked the king for being so kind to him and said goodbye to the princess who did not hear him. As he slipped from the great hall, his cat tucked under his arm, he heard the trumpets sound fortissimo and saw groups of people starting to dance.

Tom and the orange cat walked across the crinkled glass bridge that spanned the moat. Tom paused and looked back at the round, sensuous towers, minarets, and windows of the castle. He remembered in one thought the patterns in which the flowers were forced to grow, the way in which the animals were contrived to look as different as possible from their natural state and how the climate was controlled in and around the castle so that harsh winter never came.

He walked through fields of flowers and vegetables up a hill on which trees grew, bearing many various fruits. When he reached the top of the hill he had a view over the valley and saw the tarn stretching to where the sky met the water on the horizon. His lungs seemed to expand as he took in the tangy air. He strode. He noticed how he strode again; all the time he had been at the castle he had made short, careful steps across the Oriental rugs, nimble steps across the mosaics, watchful steps across the marble and cautious steps across the glass bridges. At the castle he had had to take care not to make a sudden turn and risk breaking a priceless vase, or spilling ambrosia over the glossy surface of an inlaid table.

Now he jumped into the air and seemed to hang there before landing on springy turf and swinging round, his arms carrying his body like the sails of a windmill, round and round. He fell on to the ground and laughed out loud. He lay hidden in the knee-high buttercups and daisies, flowers called weeds at the castle and uprooted if ever they dared to seed themselves in the grounds. He looked again at the hills. He looked again at the fields. Who, he wondered, had been responsible for arranging them in such perfect order and appointing them so exquisitely? The birds twittered; he thought he could never tire of their songs. The smell of rain evaporating on the warm air filled him with longing for something he could not recall. He picked himself up and walked; as he did so the artificial scents of the castle drifted from his skin. Five miles from the castle, and all the elegant stupidity, ease and mindless jollity faded like a dream fades by breakfast time.

Tom with the orange cat travelled from village to village sharpening knives, scissors, scythes, sickles and saws. It was a hard life. Tom was paid very little even though the saws he sharpened cut through logs as though they were butter and the scythes cut through thickets as if they were clouds of smoke.

For many years they trudged on foot, over the hills and down the tracks that led to the farmsteads, with all Tom owned strapped to his back. As he worked he saved. Eventually, he bought a horse and a caravan and a little later, through the generosity of a farmer, he came to own a grinder's wheel.

"There was once a grinder used to come out this way," the farmer explained. "He was a good man and a good worker. He had a hard life and he died of grief. He had had a son late in his marriage and the boy was drowned, I believe. The man could never get over it. I came by his wheel in the market. I was buying some tools and the wheel made up the lot. I stuck it in the barn; it's been there for years. Time it was used again. You take it."

Tom was delighted. He took the wheel to pieces, cleaned every part of it, oiled it and polished it and put it together again. He found it worked like a charm.

Tom's happiness was interrupted from time to time by two frustrations: he could not account for his early years and when he picked flowers he had no one to whom to give them. The first circumstance was most trying; he would like to have known who were his father and his mother, where he had lived and what sort of life he had led. The second circumstance followed from the first: he did not feel at liberty to choose a wife before he knew who his mother had been. In his bones he was satisfied his parents had been good people and he was grateful to them that he could read and write and do simple sums. There were many among the farmers and market traders he met who could not.

Since he could remember no details of his early past he was scrupulously careful to keep a record of the present. He filled books like streams are filled after the spring rains. Soon every aspect of his life found its way between the covers of a book. How he ate, what he wore, where he went, whom he met. He wrote about the seasons, the life of the birds, creatures, even the insects he encountered; he noted where he found his mushrooms and berries, set his traps, caught his fish. He kept a record of the work he did and where the farmers lived and what they paid him.

Many years passed. When he had written twenty books he knew he had been on the road for about twenty years, for each book seemed to need a full year to find its end. He was overcome by a deep longing to exchange the traveller's rootlessness for something still; for stout walls, a solid floor, a fire in a permanent grate and a door that closed against the weather. The orange cat was healthy, but very old, and spent all its days and nights curled up in a blanket. Tom knew his cat would greatly appreciate the crackle and warmth of a log fire. The caravan had served them both well, and Tom loved and respected his horse. But the horse was old and rather frail now, and the caravan suddenly seemed small and vulnerable.

It was autumn. The hills were on fire, the sky was cobalt and the barley stubble was rotting into the ground. Tom had taken his bread and cheese into the fields to eat; he wanted to enjoy the last warm rays of the autumn sun before they faded white and cool into winter. He watched a flock of birds collect in an elm, making plans for their migration to warm lands. Winter, Tom thought, is hard on birds, on creatures and on man. There are no pickings in the hedgerows; just dry sticks on the ground waiting to be burned into warmth on the fire. He was deep in thought as he drove the caravan up the lane that led to the farmhouse and the farmer's tools he had come to sharpen.

The farmer had made a pile of all that needed sharpening at one side of the yard. As Tom drove into the yard the farmer waved to him.

"Afternoon," cried out Tom.

"Afternoon," the farmer replied, adding, "Beautiful one at that!"

Tom set up his wheel outside the door of the farmhouse, and while he worked the farmer's wife brewed tea and brought it to him in a huge mug, together with a rock cake.

"I always look forward to these," Tom told her, as he bit into the cake. He worked silently and barely noticed the ducks and geese that assembled round him, fascinated by the hum of the turning wheel.

When his work was done Tom went into the

kitchen and asked the farmer's wife whether she had any kitchen knives she would like sharpened. She gave him her special chopping knife and the one she used to cut the hams. Tom swiftly put a razor edge on both and as he worked he asked her whether she knew anyone who would give him work with board and lodging.

She shook her head. "Not now the harvest's in," she said.

Tom packed his wheel into the caravan and watered his horse and was about to draw out of the farmyard when the farmer's wife called to him: "Do you mind what sort of work?" she asked.

Tom said he did not mind at all so long as it would earn him a solid roof over his head and his keep and that of his cat.

"Well," said the farmer's wife, "the blind widow on the hill will be wanting help now winter's coming. It'd be lonely up there – but then you're used to your own company. The widow's not one to talk much. I wouldn't live there," she added and shook her head against the thought. "It's bleak and dangerous by Tarn

Tegrof. Still, it might be better than nothing," she added, more cheerfully, as she wiped her hands on her apron and gave him directions.

"Follow the road out of the village towards Water's End. Two miles down and you'll see a cart track leading out into the hills. Follow the track through the barley fields and the beech wood up to the tarns. Between the tarns stands a cottage where the knife-grinder and his wife lived and worked the land. The man's been dead many years now – died of grief they say. His widow's blind, she can't work the land now. She needs a strong pair of hands and a pair of good eyes around the place. She'll see after you – cook for you, do your washing and keep a good fire in." So saying the farmer's wife turned back into her kitchen.

Tom flicked the reins against the haunches of his horse and set off down the road as he had been directed. It was five miles to the cottage that lay between the tarns. The journey could have been made in an hour and a half but Tom chose to take it slowly. He savoured the fields on the side of the hills and the moors that lay on the opposite side of the road. He watched a linnet on the gorse and a goldfinch on the thistles. He tied the horse to a post, climbed a steep escarpment just below the beech woods and looked for a long time with a hard gaze at the village of Barleymill that lay below. He felt contentment. He believed that if he looked deeply and well into the village it would give up its secrets to him.

Home! Home at last! He picked up the orange cat who had climbed slowly after him and stood with him in his arms.

It was late afternoon when Tom drew up at the widow's cottage. He looked out over the tarns. A breeze was leaning against the rushes and the mist was descending. The cat walked towards Tarn Leban. He sat looking at it as a man sits looking at a picture. Tom turned to face the cottage and liked what he saw. He knocked on the door.

"Good afternoon, ma'am. Are you after hired help?"

"Indeed, I am," the widow replied. "But how did you know?"

"The farmer's wife at Barleymill . . ." Tom started to explain, but did not have to continue.

"Ah, yes . . ." The widow drew back and pulled the door wide open, and indicated to Tom that he should come into the kitchen.

There was a smell of newly-baked bread and hot milk. Tom sat down on a chair by the side of the range and watched as the woman, her arms held out before her, with unerring judgement found all she was searching for: a bowl, bread, milk and a nutmeg. She broke the bread into pieces, she placed it in a wide bowl and over it poured hot milk. She grated nutmeg on top and handed the steaming bowl to Tom. "There now," she said, "that'll warm you."

"I have a cat," Tom told the woman and immediately she broke more bread into a bowl and over it poured the remains of the hot milk. She set the cat's bowl on the floor by the side of the range.

Tom enjoyed the hot sweet soup. He could not

remember having felt so comfortable and secure as he did now. The cat purred.

The old woman and the young man sat silent until dusk turned to dark.

"Shall I light the lamps?" Tom asked.

"I hope there's oil," replied the widow. "I've not needed light these past years so I've not bought oil."

Tom searched for oil but there was none. He lighted some candle ends he found on a window sill. Tomorrow he would bring in oil from the caravan but not tonight. He did not wish to disturb the quiet contentment by opening the door on to the now cold and windy night.

"You'll be needing the lamps," the widow continued, "you must buy oil when next you go down to Barleymill."

And so everything was settled without discussion. Tom would live at the cottage. He would manage the small-holding in return for which the widow would do his washing, cook his food and keep home for him.

The widow climbed the stairs; Tom followed her. As she climbed she said to him, "When you wake you will see from your window tarns that stretch to the east and to the west. One day, when I know you better, I'll tell you the legend of Tarn Tegrof and the gifts of Tarn Leban."

The widow opened the door on to what was to be Tom's room. It was a very simple room furnished in a manner suited to a half-grown man. There was a box bed, a rug, a straight-back chair, all neatly arranged on a polished board floor. There was a hook at the back of the door and Tom could just make out an empty lamp on a ledge by the bed. They wished each other good night. Tom and his cat slept unusually soundly and woke to see the dawn bleed through the tiny window.

It was morning. Tom stood at the door of the cottage looking out over Tarn Leban and Tarn Tegrof. He did not recognize either but he recognized the feelings that rose in him as he viewed the scene; they were familiar feelings. In his wanderings such feelings had made him restless; here the feelings rhymed with his surroundings.

"Do you have clothes in which to work?" the widow called out to Tom. "There are leather breeches and overalls in the shed. They belonged to my husband; they belong to you now."

Tom went to the shed at the side of the cottage and dressed himself in the indestructible clothes the grinder used to wear. As he did so he looked round the shed and admired the order in which the tools were arranged; the old knife-grinder had clearly been as fastidious as he. Tom returned to the kitchen where the widow was preparing his breakfast. As he came through the door she turned to face him.

"I can smell my man home again," she said, and she was pleased.

Tom worked the land during all the daylight hours; at night he and the old woman sat together by the fire, the orange cat at their feet, and Tom read from the books he had written. He learnt to address her as "Widow", as if the name were a personal one, not as familiar as a first name nor as formal as a family name but rather as he might address a man by his trade or craft. They both called the cat "Cat".

Widow asked Tom his name and he told her that he had forgotten, how some men called him "Grinder" and others called him "the traveller". I shall call you Tegrof, she said. Every time Widow called Tom "Tegrof", the terror of the tarn and the sadness it had brought her lessened.

Widow moved with such confidence Tom often forgot she was blind. She was able to knit and through the winter months she made Tom socks and sweaters. With the scraps of wool left over from these garments she crocheted blankets. She attempted everything and perfected everything. She feared only one thing: to walk alone outside the cottage yard. She put Tom in mind of an animal bound to its territory, terrified to stray from it. This puzzled Tom in a woman of such courage.

"Why will you not walk in the fields?" he would ask her.

"I prefer not to," was all she replied.

It was a sappy day in spring; blossom frothed in the trees. Widow sat at the open door of the cottage washing clean, tiny, new potatoes Tom had dug. Tom had finished work. He sat by her side and looked down the hill on the fragile green of the spring barley and watched as a lark rose sharply into the sun. Widow listened to the mallard on the tarns and regretted she would not see the ducklings when they hatched. Since her sight had failed, her hearing had become acute. She could hear squirrels building their dreys in a hole in the pine tree; she heard them as they scuttled back and forth over the ground collecting bark and sticks and digging moss to line the drey. She missed the sight of rabbits feeding and playing at dusk and early morning. Spring opened wide doors on her memories.

"Tegrof, it is time for me to tell you the legend of the tarn whose name you bear. For more than thirty years that tarn has ruled my days. When first I saw it I thought only how beautiful it looked, lying like a sheet of wrinkled glass; later I was told of its dangers and later still it robbed me of my son. It was winter, a hard winter, much harder than any we had known. Our boy, Tom, left to walk over the frozen tarn to discover its extent and what lay beyond. You will notice you cannot see to the end of the tarn . . ." Tom stared out into the far distance and agreed he could not see to the end of Tarn Tegrof.

The widow continued: "He never returned. The ice was thin round the rushes and he must have drowned. We never recovered his body; my husband took the boy's coracle on to the tarn when the ice melted and rowed out to the centre, but he dared not dive into its depths, for if anyone drinks so much as a drop of that water he forgets his very name. For years we waited, believing Tom might return, but my husband gave up hope. 'Once a child has left home,' he said, 'he does not return.' When hope left him his strength left him and he died. My hope never deserted me. I still feel Tom may return."

Tom, now called Tegrof, felt the weight of the woman's sorrow and the permanence of her faith. He determined to serve Widow for the duration of her life. "I too," said Widow, "wanted to know what lay further than the eye could see at the end of the tarn, but I was too fearful to explore. The tarn guards its secrets jealously and though a man may reach the far side, the waters conspire to rob him of his memory and wipe out his past."

Life returned to the cottage that rose between Tarn Leban and Tarn Tegrof. The land flourished abundantly. Tom worked at his grinder's wheel during the winter months but always returned to the cottage and the blind widow at night. Tom and the widow were content. The orange cat spent his time sitting at the edge of Tarn Leban remembering, perhaps, when he was young and used to fish in the generous waters.

When Widow died, as die she must, Tom buried her under a willow by the side of Tarn

Tegrof, to whose waters both had become reconciled. Tom secretly believed he had drunk of the waters but that nevertheless his life was a glorious thing. Widow never lost the memory of her son and husband and in the years of her fragility Tarn Tegrof bestowed upon her a new companion to nourish her heart, as Tarn Leban had nourished her body. When the orange cat died, shortly after Widow, Tom buried him by her side.

Tom was sad; he missed the company of his blind companion. But he accepted that the old

must die and that the young are there to continue their work. Now he felt he might marry and have children. He met a girl from Barleymill and took her to live in the cottage between the tarns.

At first she had not wanted to live in such a remote place. She was frightened by the legend of Tarn Tegrof. But Tom taught his wife that where there is love there is no place for fear. So far as it is known they and their children lived happily ever after.